FAMILY HAGGADAH

A SEDER FOR ALL GENERATIONS

הגדה של פסח

ELIE M. GINDI

COMMENTARY AND FOREWORD
RABBI LEE T. BYCEL

EDITOR
PAMELA B. SCHAFF

This Haggadah is dedicated to

Moses Elie Gindi,

who died on the first night of Passover, 1965.

———————————

May his memory be a blessing to his children

and to his children's children . . .

Copyright © 1998 Elie M. Gindi

ISBN 0-87441-685-X

Manufactured in the United States of America

(Adapted from *Family Passover Haggadah*
Copyright © 1998 EMG Publishing
PO Box 49832, Los Angeles, CA 90049)

Published by Behrman House, Inc.
235 Watchung Avenue, West Orange, New Jersey 07052

Special thanks for their invaluable help:
Carla Barr, Alissa Guttman, Justina Klimkevich, Manya Polonsky

Library of Congress Cataloging-in-Publication Data

Haggadah (Gindi). English & Hebrew.
        Family Haggadah/by Elie M. Gindi; commentary and foreword by Lee T. Bycel; edited by Pamela B.
Schaff.
        p.   cm.
        Subtitle: A Seder for All Generations.
        ISBN 0-87441-685-X
        1. Haggadah—Adaptations. 2. Jewish Families—Prayerbooks and Devotions. 3. Seder.   4.
Judaism—Prayerbooks and Devotions. I. Gindi, Elie M. II. Bycel, Lee T. III. Schaff, Pamela B. IV. Title. V.
Title: Haggadah Shel Pesah.
        BM674.795.G56   1999
        296.4'5371—dc21
                                                                                                98-54467
                                                                                                CIP
                                                                                                HE

FOREWORD

Pesach is a remarkable holiday. Its main celebration is in the home. The seder allows us to experience both slavery and freedom, as we tell young people a story that is at once ancient and modern. We eat a wonderful meal, visit with friends and family, discuss contemporary issues, and sing songs. The Haggadah is our guide through the seder. This Haggadah was created for seders that include people of all ages; the story is told in a manner in which children can freely participate. An initial section on preparing for the seder provides useful hints and ideas for the leader. Text boxes with guiding questions and engaging commentary are scattered throughout, encouraging thoughtful discussion. The description of sources following the text provides informative background regarding each image.

The unique aspect of this Haggadah is its tribute to illuminated Haggadot throughout the ages. For many centuries, artists have interpreted the Passover story through their creative works. Elie M. Gindi conveys this compelling story with an approachable text and specially selected reproductions of images from these magnificent Haggadot, along with captivating pictures of young people enacting parts of the seder. This radiant and colorful Haggadah encourages the participant to experience the seder not simply through words, but through a feast of rich and vibrant images.

My family and I were privileged to be present when this Haggadah was first introduced in experimental form. I will never forget the sparkling eyes of the children and adults as they turned from page to page, discovering another print from an illuminated Haggadah. This elegant volume invites all participants to experience fully the Pesach story. The captivating pictures, combined with the story rendered in a friendly and readable manner, create a Haggadah that will help you teach the mysteries of Pesach while uplifting the spirits of all at the Passover table.

Rabbi Lee T. Bycel

PREPARING FOR THE SEDER

Passover is a family holiday. It's a good idea to read and tell Passover stories to children before the holiday arrives. Encourage children to prepare for the seder: help them create art objects or seder plates, have them practice the Four Questions, the "Mah Nishtanah," ask them to prepare an answer to a seder question, or help them design a skit or appropriate costume. On the night of the seder, you can sing songs and tell stories that the children know. You can also prepare quiet table activities, such as puzzles and matching games, to keep them occupied and interested.

In this Haggadah, colorful images surround a concise, readable text, with shaded boxes that include questions, interesting facts, or topics for discussion. The leader chooses which boxes to include and sets the pace for the seder. Important concepts when formulating an overall seder plan include:

◊ Keep within a reasonable time period. The seder using this Haggadah should take approximately 45 minutes before and 15 minutes after the meal, though this may vary depending on the amount of discussion.
◊ Gauge the level of discussion to keep the interest of the participants.
◊ Decide on a format that will encourage questions and discussion.

The ideal environment is one of comfort (reclining is suggested), where those present freely participate in the reading of the Haggadah and in the resulting discussion. The spirit of Passover is to include individuals with whom you might not ordinarily dine, Jews or non-Jews. Those with curiosity about the holiday and its traditions are excellent candidates. It's a mitzvah to invite someone in need.

SEDER CHECKLIST

◊ Haggadot
◊ seder plate
◊ holiday candles
◊ cup for Elijah (to be filled with wine)
◊ cup for Miriam (to be filled with water)
◊ cup, basin, and towels for handwashing
◊ wine cup for each person
◊ small plates for symbolic foods
◊ matzah cover or bag
◊ pillows for reclining
◊ kids' projects, playful items, and props

◊ wine (some substitute grape juice)
◊ matzot: for participants, three to be covered, and an extra "Matzah of Hope"
◊ roasted egg for the seder plate, hard-boiled eggs for participants – "Beitzah"
◊ parsley or celery – "Karpas"
◊ roasted bone (lamb, chicken, or beet) – "Zeroa"
◊ horseradish, bitter lettuce, or bitter vegetable for the bitter herb – "Maror"
◊ romaine or other bitter lettuce – "Chazeret"
◊ charoset (mixture of apples, nuts, wine, and spices; some use dates, nuts, and wine)
◊ salt water for dipping

Searching for chametz, from the *Second Cincinnati Haggadah*, Amsterdam, ca. 1716

SEARCHING FOR CHAMETZ

Children often enjoy the ritual of searching for and disposing of chametz, the term for leavened food (food and drink made from grains such as wheat, barley, rye, oats, or their derivatives that have been allowed to leaven). The night before Passover, gather the children with the necessary tools: a candle, a feather, and a spoon. Ahead of time, place some bread around the search area. Turn the lights off and allow the children to find the chametz by candlelight. They will scoop up the crumbs by using the feather and the spoon.

Recite the following biblical passage and prayer:

"Remember this day as the day you left Egypt, from the house of slavery. It was with a mighty hand that God led you out. No chametz should be eaten." (Exodus 13:3)

בָּרוּךְ אַתָּה יְיָ אֱלֹהֵינוּ מֶלֶךְ הָעוֹלָם אֲשֶׁר קִדְּשָׁנוּ בְּמִצְוֹתָיו וְצִוָּנוּ עַל בְּעוּר חָמֵץ.

Ba-ruch a-tah A-do-nai E-lo-hey-nu me-lech ha-o-lam a-sher kid'sha-nu b'mitz-vo-tav v'tzi-va-nu al bi-ur cha-metz.

Blessed are You, Eternal God, Ruler of the Universe, who has sanctified us with laws and commanded us to remove chametz from our homes.

THE SEDER

This book is a Haggadah. Haggadah means "telling." By reading the words of the Haggadah we tell the story of Pesach, the Hebrew word for Passover. "Pass over" refers to the tenth plague that befell Egypt but passed over Israelite homes. Our ceremony for Passover is called the seder, which means "order." Through this traditionally ordered ritual, we will retell the story of the Israelites' journey from slavery in Egypt to freedom in the Promised Land, eat special foods that symbolize Passover's many messages, and teach our children the traditions of Pesach, first celebrated more than 3,000 years ago.

Telling the story of Passover is one of the most important mitzvot in Jewish life. As the Torah tells us, "You shall tell the Pesach story to your children in the days to come." (Exodus 13:8)

Tonight's seder is not just the retelling of an ancient and compelling story. Rather, we are asked actually to experience the bitterness of oppression and the sweetness of freedom so we may better understand the hope and courage of all men and women, of all generations, in their quest for liberty, security, and human rights.

An ancient rabbinic text instructs us, "Each person in every generation must regard himself or herself as having been personally freed from Egypt." (Mishnah Pesachim)

We have before us family and friends, a beautifully prepared table, a great feast, and a traditionally arranged seder plate. Let us recline, enjoy, learn, and relive the dramatic and miraculous Pesach.

❓ Jews have celebrated Pesach for more than 120 generations. How many generations of people are at your seder table?

"Ha lachma anya," the traditional first three words of the Haggadah, mean: "This is the bread of affliction."

From the *Spanish Haggadah*, ca. 1350-60

CANDLELIGHTING

B efore the seder begins, we light and recite the blessing over the festival candles. In the Jewish tradition, the day begins and ends at sunset. These candles symbolize the transition to a new day and remind us that Passover is a holy time.

(On Sabbath add words in brackets)

בָּרוּךְ אַתָּה יְיָ אֱלֹהֵינוּ
מֶלֶךְ הָעוֹלָם אֲשֶׁר קִדְּשָׁנוּ
בְּמִצְוֹתָיו וְצִוָּנוּ לְהַדְלִיק נֵר
שֶׁל [שַׁבָּת וְשֶׁל] יוֹם טוֹב.

Ba-ruch a-tah A-do-nai E-lo-hey-nu
me-lech ha-o-lam a-sher kid'sha-nu
b'mitz-vo-tav v'tzi-va-nu l'had-lik ner
shel (Shabbat v'shel) Yom Tov.

Blessed are You, Eternal God, Ruler of the Universe, who has sanctified us with laws and commanded us to light the (Sabbath and) holiday candles.

> ? How is your seder table the same or different from the one in this scene?

From *Haggadah for Passover*, 1921

THE ORDER

PARTICIPANT:

There are 14 steps in the order of our seder.

1. KADESH
קַדֵּשׁ

The Blessing

2. URCHATZ
וּרְחַץ

Handwashing

3. KARPAS
כַּרְפַּס

The Greens

4. YACHATZ
יַחַץ

Breaking the Middle
Matzah

5. MAGGID
מַגִּיד

Telling the Story

6. ROCHTZAH
רָחְצָה

Second Handwashing

7. MOTZI MATZAH
מוֹצִיא מַצָּה

Blessing for the
Matzah

14. NIRTZAH
נִרְצָה

Conclusion

13. HALLEL
הַלֵּל

Praising God

12. BARECH
בָּרֵךְ

Blessing after
the Meal

11. TZAFUN
צָפוּן

The Afikoman

10. SHULCHAN ORECH
שֻׁלְחָן עוֹרֵךְ

The Meal

✡ If there are children
at your table who
made seder plates or other
seder symbols, now would
be a good time for them to
share their creative work.

9. KORECH
כּוֹרֵךְ

Hillel's Sandwich

8. MAROR
מָרוֹר

The Bitter Herbs

4

THE SEDER PLATE

On our table is the seder plate on which are six symbolic foods:

THE ZEROA, a roasted shankbone, reminds us of the special lamb that was brought to the Temple in Jerusalem on Passover as an offering to God.

THE BEITZAH, a boiled egg, is smooth and round and symbolizes the new life that comes with springtime.

MAROR, a bitter herb, reminds us of the bitterness of Egyptian bondage.

CHAROSET, a mixture of wine, nuts, and pulp, represents the mortar our ancestors used in building cities in the land of the pyramids.

KARPAS, a green vegetable, reminds us that Passover occurs during springtime when new life brings a feeling of hope.

Tiered seder plate, Vienna, 1814

CHAZERET, the bitter herb used in a sandwich, follows the custom established by Hillel, a wise rabbi and teacher, to remind us that our ancestors ate matzah and bitter herbs together.

1. KADESH — The Blessing
קַדֵּשׁ

Participant:

Wine symbolizes the "joy of life." Tonight we drink wine four times during the seder, representing God's four promises to the Israelites of redemption from slavery, which are mentioned in the Book of Exodus (Chapter 13):

1. "I will free you."
2. "I will deliver you."
3. "I will redeem you."
4. "I will take you to be My people."

> Wine is a symbol of sanctification in Jewish life. In Jewish thought, no object or action is intrinsically good or bad. Its value is in the way it is used or misused.

PARTICIPANT:

With the first cup of wine we recall the first promise found in the Torah, "I am Adonai, and I will free you from slavery in Egypt."

בָּרוּךְ אַתָּה יְיָ אֱלֹהֵינוּ
מֶלֶךְ הָעוֹלָם בּוֹרֵא פְּרִי הַגָּפֶן.

Ba-ruch a-tah A-do-nai E-lo-hey-nu me-lech ha-o-lam bo-rey p'ri ha-ga-fen.

Blessed are You, Eternal God, Ruler of the Universe, who creates the fruit of the vine.

(On Sabbath add words in brackets)

בָּרוּךְ אַתָּה יְיָ אֱלֹהֵינוּ מֶלֶךְ הָעוֹלָם אֲשֶׁר
בָּחַר בָּנוּ מִכָּל־עָם וְרוֹמְמָנוּ מִכָּל־לָשׁוֹן
וְקִדְּשָׁנוּ בְּמִצְוֹתָיו. וַתִּתֶּן־לָנוּ יְיָ אֱלֹהֵינוּ
בְּאַהֲבָה [שַׁבָּתוֹת לִמְנוּחָה וּ]מוֹעֲדִים לְשִׂמְחָה,
חַגִּים וּזְמַנִּים לְשָׂשׂוֹן, אֶת־יוֹם [הַשַּׁבָּת הַזֶּה,
וְאֶת־יוֹם] חַג הַמַּצּוֹת הַזֶּה, זְמַן חֵרוּתֵנוּ,
[בְּאַהֲבָה] מִקְרָא קֹדֶשׁ זֵכֶר לִיצִיאַת
מִצְרָיִם. כִּי בָנוּ בָחַרְתָּ וְאוֹתָנוּ קִדַּשְׁתָּ
מִכָּל־הָעַמִּים [וְשַׁבָּת] וּמוֹעֲדֵי קָדְשֶׁךָ
[בְּאַהֲבָה וּבְרָצוֹן] בְּשִׂמְחָה וּבְשָׂשׂוֹן
הִנְחַלְתָּנוּ. בָּרוּךְ אַתָּה יְיָ מְקַדֵּשׁ
[הַשַּׁבָּת וְ]יִשְׂרָאֵל וְהַזְּמַנִּים.

From *The Haggadah*
Arthur Szyk, 1965

Blessed are You, Eternal God, for selecting us as being worthy of Your covenant, and for sanctifying us through Your commandments. In Your love, You have given us (Sabbaths for rest,) festivals for rejoicing, holidays, and seasons of joy, including this festival of Passover, the time of our freedom, (in love) the sacred occasion commemorating the Exodus from Egypt. Blessed are You, Eternal God, who sanctifies (the Sabbath,) Your people Israel, and the festivals.

SHEHECHEYANU

ALL:

בָּרוּךְ אַתָּה יְיָ אֱלֹהֵינוּ מֶלֶךְ הָעוֹלָם שֶׁהֶחֱיָנוּ
וְקִיְּמָנוּ וְהִגִּיעָנוּ לַזְּמַן הַזֶּה.

Ba-ruch a-tah A-do-nai E-lo-hey-nu me-lech ha-o-lam she-he-che-ya-nu, v'kiy'ma-nu, v'hi-giy-a-nu, laz-man ha-zeh.

Blessed are You, Eternal God, Ruler of the Universe, who has kept us alive and sustained us and allowed us to reach this season.

All drink the first cup of wine while reclining.

2. URCHATZ — Handwashing
וּרְחַץ

LEADER:

We wash our hands as a way of getting ready. During Urchatz we do not say a blessing. We are free to wash, recline, read, remember, learn, and teach.

The leader of the seder pours water over both hands.

3. KARPAS — The Greens
כַּרְפַּס

PARTICIPANT WHO WAS BORN IN SPRINGTIME:

We remember that it was springtime when the Passover story took place. As we dip greens in salt water, we remember the tears of our ancestors who suffered as slaves in Egypt and the tears of those who still are not free today.

SONG OF SONGS 2:10-12

Arise, my beloved, my fair one,
And come away;
For lo, the winter is past,
Flowers appear on the earth,
The time of singing is here.
The song of the dove
Is heard in our land.

Let us go down to the vineyards
To see if the vines have budded.
There will I give You my love.

From the *First Cincinnati Haggadah*,
Southern Germany, ca.1480–90

> ❓ What signs of springtime have you seen so far this year? What else can you expect?

We dip parsley, celery, or lettuce in salt water and recite the prayer.

ALL:

בָּרוּךְ אַתָּה יְיָ אֱלֹהֵינוּ מֶלֶךְ הָעוֹלָם בּוֹרֵא פְּרִי הָאֲדָמָה.

Ba-ruch a-tah A-do-nai E-lo-hey-nu me-lech ha-o-lam bo-rey p'ri ha-a-da-mah.

Blessed are You, Eternal God, Ruler of the Universe, who creates the fruit of the earth.

7

4. YACHATZ — Breaking the Middle Matzah
יַחַץ

The leader uncovers the three matzot, takes the middle one, breaks it in two, wraps up the larger part, and sets it aside for the afikoman (the symbolic seder dessert). The leader takes the smaller part, replaces it in the middle, and wraps them all in a sack. In the Sephardic tradition, each willing participant slings the sack over his or her shoulder.

ALL: "Mi attah?" – Who are you?
PARTICIPANT: "Ani Yehudi." – I am a Jew.
ALL: From where are you coming?
PARTICIPANT: From Egypt.
ALL: And where are you going?
PARTICIPANT: To Jerusalem.

The matzot are placed back on the seder plate and the afikoman is hidden.

Matzah comb,
Germany, 18th-19th century

✡ Why do we hide the larger piece of matzah? Some say it is because more is hidden than revealed. We ask questions and seek out the hidden messages of this special holiday.

5. MAGGID — Telling the Story
מַגִּיד

Matzah bag,
Moravia, 1904

The leader lifts up a (fourth) piece of matzah.

LEADER:

This matzah is the "Matzah of Hope." We set it aside as a symbol of hope for those Jews throughout the world who are not free to celebrate Passover.

Each participant lifts up a piece of matzah.

ALL:

הָא לַחְמָא עַנְיָא — *Ha lach-ma an-ya*

This is the bread of affliction which our
     ancestors ate in the land of Egypt.
Let all those who are hungry come and
     eat with us.
Let all those who are in need come and
     share our meal.
This year we are here.
This year we are still slaves.
Next year may we all be free.

❓ Are there still people who are not free? In what ways are they still enslaved?

The matzot are covered.
The second cup of wine is filled.

THE FOUR QUESTIONS

מַה נִּשְׁתַּנָּה הַלַּיְלָה הַזֶּה מִכָּל־הַלֵּילוֹת?

שֶׁבְּכָל־הַלֵּילוֹת אָנוּ אוֹכְלִין חָמֵץ וּמַצָּה. הַלַּיְלָה הַזֶּה כֻּלּוֹ מַצָּה.

שֶׁבְּכָל־הַלֵּילוֹת אָנוּ אוֹכְלִין שְׁאָר יְרָקוֹת. הַלַּיְלָה הַזֶּה מָרוֹר.

שֶׁבְּכָל־הַלֵּילוֹת אֵין אָנוּ מַטְבִּילִין אֲפִילוּ פַּעַם אֶחָת. הַלַּיְלָה הַזֶּה שְׁתֵּי פְעָמִים.

שֶׁבְּכָל־הַלֵּילוֹת אָנוּ אוֹכְלִין בֵּין יוֹשְׁבִין וּבֵין מְסֻבִּין. הַלַּיְלָה הַזֶּה כֻּלָּנוּ מְסֻבִּין.

From *The Haggadah*, Arthur Szyk, 1965

Mah nish-ta-nah ha-lai-lah ha-zeh mi-kol ha-lay-lot?
She-b'chol ha-lay-lot a-nu och'leen cha-maytz u-ma-tzah.
Ha-lai-lah ha-zeh ku-lo ma-tzah.

She-b'chol ha-lay-lot a-nu och'leen sh'ar y'ra-kot.
Ha-lai-lah ha-zeh ma-ror.

She-b'chol ha-lay-lot ayn a-nu mat-bi-lin a-fi-lu pa-am e-chat.
Ha-lai-lah ha-zeh sh'tay f'a-mim.

She-b'chol ha-lay-lot a-nu och'leen bayn yosh-veen u-vayn m'su-bin.
Ha-lai-lah ha-zeh ku-la-nu m'su-bin.

> ✡ "Mah Nishtanah,"
> The Four Questions,
> is traditionally recited by
> the youngest at the table.

How does this night differ from all other nights?

On all other nights we eat either leavened or unleavened bread. Why on this night do we eat only unleavened bread?

On all other nights we eat all kinds of herbs. Why on this night do we eat only bitter herbs?

On all other nights we need not dip our herbs even once. Why on this night do we need to dip twice?

On all other nights we eat sitting or reclining. Why on this night do we recline?

THE ANSWERS

The matzot are uncovered.

PARTICIPANT:

This night is different from all other nights because of our unique celebration of freedom. We eat only matzah to highlight the tale of our hasty exodus from Egypt.

We eat bitter herbs so that we too may sample at least a taste of bitterness.

We dip our bitter herbs twice, once in salt water and once in sweet charoset, as we remember both the salty tears of our ancestors and the sweetness of their hope for freedom.

As a symbol of our comfort, we recline and eat as free men and women.

From *Passover Haggadah*, Darmstadt, Germany, 1733

PARTICIPANT:

A tale is told about five rabbis on a Passover evening during the beginning of the second century of the Common Era. While reclining at a seder, they told and retold the story of the Exodus from Egypt all through the night. One of their disciples came running to tell them, "It's time to read the morning Sh'ma, the time for morning prayers." These five sages, even though well versed in the story, had reviewed the story over and over again, suggesting that they wanted to savor every nuance of the narrative. This evening, we too are discovering new meanings as we retell this ancient story.

Avadim Hayinu

no capo
Allegro

A-va-dim ha-yi-nu, ha-yi - nu. A-tah b' nai cho-rin,_____ b'
nai cho - rin. A - va - dim ha - yi-nu. A-
tah, a-tah b' nai cho - rin.____ A - va - dim____
ha - yi - nu____ a-tah, a-tah b' nai cho-rin, b' nai cho - rin.

PARTICIPANT:

We were all slaves to Pharaoh in Egypt. And Adonai our God delivered us with a mighty hand and an outstretched arm. If God had not brought our ancestors out of Egypt, then we, our children, and our children's children would have remained slaves. So, even if all of us were scholars, full of understanding and wisdom, and learned in Torah, it would still be our obligation to tell the story of how we left Egypt. Everyone who studies the meaning of the Exodus from Egypt deserves praise.

✡ This beautiful and ancient song is a remarkable, timeless allegory. We realize that pharaohs are not the only oppressive leaders, Egypt is not the only place where people feel trapped, and the Israelites are not the only ones seeking and struggling to obtain freedom. We celebrate and relive our Exodus not only to remember our enslavement, but also to highlight the manner in which we were freed. We are inspired to consider how we can protect and assure the freedom of all people.

From the *Barcelona Haggadah*, Barcelona, mid-14th century

IN EVERY GENERATION

בְּכָל־דּוֹר וָדוֹר חַיָּב אָדָם לִרְאוֹת אֶת־עַצְמוֹ
כְּאִלּוּ הוּא יָצָא מִמִּצְרָיִם.

B'chol dor va-dor cha-yav a-dam lir'ot et atz-mo k'i-lu hu ya-tza mi-Mitz-ra-yim.

Each person in every generation must regard himself or herself as
having been personally freed from Egypt.

> **?** Which parts
> of the Passover
> story do you see in the
> pictures below?

From *The Golden Haggadah*, Spain, probably Barcelona, ca. 1320

THE FOUR CHILDREN (Pam's favorite part)

LEADER:

 As you read the Haggadah, identify your favorite part.

The Torah commands us four times to teach our children about the Exodus from Egypt. Rabbis have said there are four kinds of children, each of whom learns in a different way. Our challenge is to find the answers that best respond to each child's questions.

PARTICIPANT:

The **wise child** asks, "What is the meaning of the laws of Pesach?" This eager child has a thirst for knowledge and is told all that he or she may grasp in the experience of the seder.

"The Four Sons," from *Song of David / The Moss Haggadah*, David Moss, 1980

PARTICIPANT:

The **defiant child** asks, "What does this celebration mean to *you*?" This isolated child does not include himself or herself in the question and acts like a stranger at the seder. We challenge this child's defiance by saying, "Had you been in Egypt at the time of the Exodus, you would not have been included when God freed our ancestors from slavery." The invitation to learn and participate in the seder remains open, reflecting the belief that we all have the ability to change.

PARTICIPANT:

The **simple child** asks, "What is this all about?" We teach this unpretentious and impressionable child about the story of Exodus in terms that he or she may understand. We afford this child all the attention needed to grasp what is within his or her capacity.

PARTICIPANT:

There is a **child who does not know how to ask.** We entertain this young child with the settings on the seder table. Let this child's imagination flourish, inspired by the things on the table.

13

THE STORY

CHILD:

Many years ago, long before any of us was born, there was a wicked king called Pharaoh who ruled in the land of Egypt. Many Israelites lived there peacefully with the Egyptians. Pharaoh was afraid there were too many Israelites and that they were becoming too powerful. He commanded that they become slaves and forced them to build cities and palaces for him. Even Israelite children had to work for Pharaoh. Pharaoh and his men shouted:

From *The Haggadah of Passover*, Sigmund Forst, 1955

YOUNGEST CHILDREN:

BANG, BANG, BANG...
HOLD YOUR HAMMER LOW.
BANG, BANG, BANG...
GIVE A HEAVY BLOW.

FOR IT'S WORK, WORK, WORK...
EVERY DAY AND EVERY NIGHT.
FOR IT'S WORK, WORK, WORK...
WHEN IT'S DARK AND WHEN
    IT'S LIGHT.

DIG, DIG, DIG...
GET YOUR SHOVEL DEEP.
DIG, DIG, DIG...
THERE'S NO TIME FOR SLEEP.

FOR IT'S WORK, WORK, WORK...
EVERY DAY AND EVERY NIGHT.
FOR IT'S WORK, WORK, WORK...
WHEN IT'S DARK AND WHEN
    IT'S LIGHT.

Bang, Bang, Bang

Pharaoh was mean to Israelite adults and children. Wicked Pharaoh did not want Israelite children to grow to be adults. One Israelite mother was afraid and wanted to protect her child from Pharaoh and his men. She put her baby in a basket made of reeds and placed him by the River Nile. Pharaoh's daughter, the princess, was bathing in the river and found the baby. She brought him to her palace and named him Moses, which means "pulled from the water." The princess knew Moses was an Israelite, but she kept it a secret and raised him as a prince.

From *Haggadah of Passover*, Dr. Joseph Loewy & Joseph Guens, Tel Aviv, after 1945

CHILD:

As Moses grew to be a man, he found out that he was an Israelite and he saw how cruel Pharaoh was. One day he saw an Egyptian beating a slave, became angry, and killed the Egyptian. Afraid for his life, Moses fled Egypt and became a shepherd in a faraway land.

One day, while tending his sheep, Moses saw a bush that was on fire but that was not burning up. From the bush came God's voice. The voice told Moses to go back to Egypt to free the Children of Israel and take them far away. Moses returned to Egypt and went to see Pharaoh. Moses said to Pharaoh, "If you do not free the Children of Israel, you shall be punished." The wicked king did not believe Moses and said, "No." God was angry with Pharaoh and punished him and the Egyptians ten times. These punishments are called the ten plagues.

Let My People Go, from "The Story of Exodus" series,
Marc Chagall, Jerusalem, 1967

Let My People Go

16

THE TEN PLAGUES

LEADER:

These are the plagues that God brought upon the Egyptians in Egypt. Now as we mention each plague, we will spill some wine. We must acknowledge that all people are God's creatures and that our joy is lessened when anyone, even our enemy, suffers.

Leader or participants spill out a drop of wine as each plague is mentioned.

דָם

1. BLOOD

צְפַרְדֵעַ

2. FROGS

כִּנִּים

3. LICE

עָרוֹב

4. BEASTS

דֶבֶר

5. CATTLE DISEASE

מַכַּת בְּכוֹרוֹת

10. SLAYING
OF THE
FIRSTBORN

חֹשֶׁךְ

9. DARKNESS

אַרְבֶּה

8. LOCUSTS

בָּרָד

7. HAIL

שְׁחִין

6. BOILS

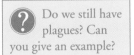
? Do we still have plagues? Can you give an example?

רבת!
RIBBIT

CHILDREN:

ONE MORNING, KING PHARAOH
WOKE UP IN HIS BED.
THERE WERE FROGS IN HIS BED
AND FROGS ON HIS HEAD.
FROGS ON HIS NOSE, AND FROGS
ON HIS TOES,
FROGS HERE, FROGS THERE,
FROGS WERE JUMPING EVERYWHERE!

CHILD:

At last, Pharaoh was frightened and let the Israelites go. They hurried out of Egypt, without time to bake bread for their journey. Instead, they put raw dough on their backs, which the sun baked into hard crackers called matzot. The Children of Israel followed Moses to the edge of the Sea of Reeds, and God divided the sea.

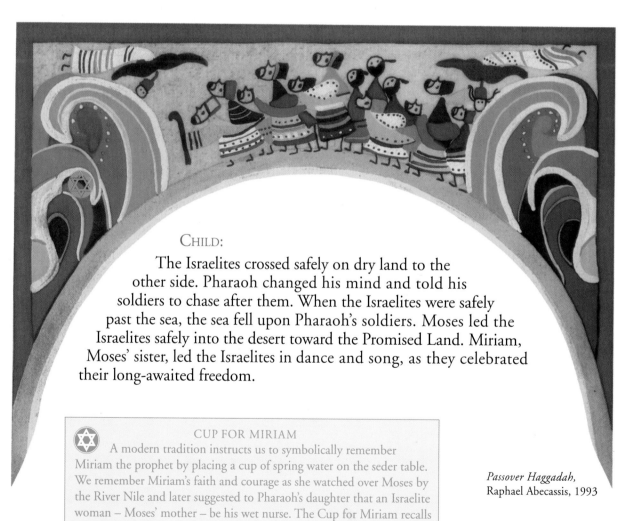

CHILD:

The Israelites crossed safely on dry land to the other side. Pharaoh changed his mind and told his soldiers to chase after them. When the Israelites were safely past the sea, the sea fell upon Pharaoh's soldiers. Moses led the Israelites safely into the desert toward the Promised Land. Miriam, Moses' sister, led the Israelites in dance and song, as they celebrated their long-awaited freedom.

> ✡ **CUP FOR MIRIAM**
> A modern tradition instructs us to symbolically remember Miriam the prophet by placing a cup of spring water on the seder table. We remember Miriam's faith and courage as she watched over Moses by the River Nile and later suggested to Pharaoh's daughter that an Israelite woman – Moses' mother – be his wet nurse. The Cup for Miriam recalls a midrash (rabbinic commentary) that wherever our ancestors wandered in the Sinai wilderness, Miriam's Well would appear and sustain them.

Passover Haggadah,
Raphael Abecassis, 1993

CHILD:

On their journey that would lead them to the Promised Land, the Children of Israel entered into a covenant, an agreement, with God at Mount Sinai and received the Commandments. They had many children, and their children had many children. As Jews, we are descendants of these families.

The 14th-century *Sarajevo Haggadah* accompanied the Jews expelled from Spain in 1492. It remained in Sarajevo with one family until the 19th century, when they sold it to the National Museum. Hidden from the Nazis in a peasant hut, it later miraculously survived the Bosnian War, when many other ancient manuscripts were destroyed.

From the *Sarajevo Haggadah,* Barcelona, 14th century

LEADER:

According to the Mishnah, the ancient code of Jewish law, Rabbi Gamliel said: "Whoever does not consider the meaning of these three, **PESACH, MATZAH, MAROR,** has not fulfilled the purpose of the seder." (Pesachim 10:5)

The leader points to each symbol as it is mentioned.

ALL:

PESACH, a shankbone, is a reminder that God "passed over" the houses of our ancestors in Egypt during the tenth plague.

MATZAH is meant to recall our hasty flight from Egypt. We fulfill the mitzvah, "For seven days you shall eat matzah, that you may remember your departure from Egypt as long as you live." (Exodus 12:15)

MAROR, the bitter herb, is the symbol of the bitterness of servitude. May we have sympathy for all who are enslaved because of their heredity, environment, or self-imposed limitations.

Let us take a moment to remember our brothers and sisters who have been enslaved at various times in history and those who are still not free today. The following is a poem written by an 11-year-old boy while he was in the Terezin concentration camp during World War II.

I AM A JEW

I am a Jew and will be a Jew forever.
Even if I should die from hunger,
never will I submit.
I will always fight for my people,
on my honor.
I will never be ashamed of them,
I give my word.

I am proud of my people,
how dignified they are.
Even though I am suppressed,
I will always come back to life.

Franta Bass
(from *I Never Saw Another Butterfly*,
edited by Hana Volavkova, 1993
Schocken Books, Inc., New York)

During the Holocaust, Jews still celebrated Passover but often had to eat bread, as matzah was unavailable. The Jews in the Warsaw Ghetto said a special prayer asking God for permission to eat bread: "Our prayer to You is that You may keep us alive and save us and rescue us speedily so that we may observe Your commandments and do Your will and serve You with a perfect heart." Amen.

From the *Birds' Head Haggadah*, Southern Germany, ca. 1300

DAYENU

PARTICIPANT:

Dayenu means, "It would have been enough for us." The meaning of this hymn is that any one of the things God did for us, as mentioned in each verse, would have been enough to deserve our gratitude.

אִלוּ הוֹצִיאָנוּ מִמִּצְרַיִם - דַּיֵנוּ

I-lu ho-tzi-a-nu mi-Mitz'ra-yim — Dayenu

Had God only taken us out of Egypt — Dayenu

אִלוּ נָתַן לָנוּ אֶת הַשַׁבָּת - דַּיֵנוּ

I-lu na-tan la-nu et ha-Shab-bat — Dayenu

Had God only given us Shabbat — Dayenu

אִלוּ נָתַן לָנוּ אֶת הַתּוֹרָה - דַּיֵנוּ

I-lu na-tan la-nu et ha-To-rah — Dayenu

Had God only given us the Torah — Dayenu

אִלוּ הִכְנִיסָנוּ לְאֶרֶץ יִשְׂרָאֵל - דַּיֵנוּ

I-lu hich'niy-sa-nu l'E-retz Yis-ra-el — Dayenu

Had God only brought us to the Land of Israel — Dayenu

ALL:

We recall God's second promise, "I will deliver you from bondage."

בָּרוּךְ אַתָּה יְיָ אֱלֹהֵינוּ מֶלֶךְ הָעוֹלָם בּוֹרֵא פְּרִי הַגָּפֶן.

Ba-ruch a-tah A-do-nai E-lo-hey-nu me-lech ha-o-lam bo-rey p'ri ha-ga-fen.

Blessed are You, Eternal God, Ruler of the Universe, who creates the fruit of the vine.

All drink the second cup of wine.

6. ROCHTZAH — Second Handwashing

רָחְצָה

LEADER:

We wash our hands in preparation for eating the matzah. This time we say a blessing.

בָּרוּךְ אַתָּה יְיָ אֱלֹהֵינוּ מֶלֶךְ הָעוֹלָם אֲשֶׁר קִדְּשָׁנוּ
בְּמִצְוֹתָיו וְצִוָּנוּ עַל נְטִילַת יָדָיִם.

*Ba-ruch a-tah A-do-nai E-lo-hey-nu me-lech ha-o-lam a-sher kid'sha-nu
b'mitz-vo-tav v'tzi-va-nu al n'ti-lat ya-da-yim.*

Blessed are You, Eternal God, Ruler of the Universe, who has sanctified
us with laws and commanded us to wash our hands.

All pour water over their hands using the cup and basin.

7. MOTZI MATZAH — Blessing for the Matzah
מוֹצִיא מַצָּה

The leader lifts the three matzot.

ALL:

בָּרוּךְ אַתָּה יְיָ אֱלֹהֵינוּ מֶלֶךְ
הָעוֹלָם הַמּוֹצִיא לֶחֶם מִן הָאָרֶץ.

*Ba-ruch a-tah A-do-nai E-lo-hey-nu me-lech
ha-o-lam ha-mo-tzi le-chem min ha-a-retz.*

Blessed are You, Eternal God, Ruler of the
Universe, who brings forth bread from the earth.

ALL:

בָּרוּךְ אַתָּה יְיָ אֱלֹהֵינוּ מֶלֶךְ
הָעוֹלָם אֲשֶׁר קִדְּשָׁנוּ בְּמִצְוֹתָיו
וְצִוָּנוּ עַל אֲכִילַת מַצָּה.

*Ba-ruch a-tah A-do-nai E-lo-hey-nu me-lech
ha-o-lam a-sher kid'sha-nu b'mitz-vo-tav
v'tzi-va-nu al a-chi-lat ma-tzah.*

Blessed are You, Eternal God, Ruler of the
Universe, who has sanctified us with laws
and commanded us to eat matzah.

Matzah cover,
Jerusalem, early 20th century

*The bottom matzah is put back in its place. The top and
middle matzot are distributed. All eat matzah while
reclining.*

IF MATZAH ISN'T YOUR FAVORITE FOOD, RECITE:

This is the poorest, the driest of bread.
It crinkles and crumbles all over our beds.
This is the matzah that Grand-Daddy ate
When he zoomed out of Egypt, afraid he'd be late.
You're welcome to join us—Come one or come many!
I'll give you my matzah. I sure don't want any.

From *Uncle Eli's Haggadah*,
Eliezer Segal, 1998
No Starch Press, San Francisco

HANG IN, FOOD SOON!

IF YOU LIKE MATZAH, ADD THESE LINES:

But tomorrow you'll smear it with butter and jelly
And then you'll enjoy as it fills up your belly.

8. MAROR — The Bitter Herbs
מָרוֹר

PARTICIPANT:

Let us each dip a piece of maror into charoset as we recall the bitterness of slavery. We recite the blessing.

בָּרוּךְ אַתָּה יְיָ אֱלֹהֵינוּ מֶלֶךְ הָעוֹלָם אֲשֶׁר קִדְּשָׁנוּ
בְּמִצְוֹתָיו וְצִוָּנוּ עַל אֲכִילַת מָרוֹר.

*Ba-ruch a-tah A-do-nai E-lo-hey-nu me-lech ha-o-lam a-sher
kid'sha-nu b'mitz-vo-tav v'tzi-va-nu al a-chi-lat ma-ror.*

Blessed are You, Eternal God, Ruler of the Universe, who has sanctified
us with laws and commanded us to eat bitter herbs.

All dip the bitter herbs in charoset and eat while reclining.

According to a midrash, enslaved Israelites called Pharaoh "Maror" because he embittered their lives.

Making Haroset, Toby Knobel Fluek, Czernica, Poland, 1975

9. KORECH — Hillel's Sandwich
כּוֹרֵךְ

PARTICIPANT:

When the ancient Temple still stood, Hillel would make a sandwich of matzah and maror and eat it together with charoset. The charoset reminds us of the mortar used to glue the bricks together when we built Pharaoh's cities.

The bottom matzah is distributed for Hillel's sandwich. Take a piece of matzah and break it into two pieces. Add the chazeret, the second kind of bitter herb, as the middle of the sandwich, dip the sandwich into charoset, and eat it while reclining . . . in one mouthful, if you dare.

THE SHANKBONE (Zeroa)

In the Sephardic tradition, pieces of meat from the shankbone are eaten by each participant. In the Ashkenazic tradition, the shankbone is acknowledged but not eaten.

PARTICIPANT:

The Torah speaks of God's outstretched arm (*zeroa*). The shankbone helps us remember God's might. The shankbone reminds us, too, of the special lamb that was brought to the Temple in Jerusalem on Passover as an offering to God.

THE EGG (Beitzah)

It is customary to start off our meal with a boiled egg dipped in salt or salt water.

PARTICIPANT:

We remember the new life the Children of Israel made for themselves when they left slavery so long ago.

First Seder in Jerusalem, Reuven Rubin, Tel Aviv, 1950

10. SHULCHAN ORECH — The Meal
שֻׁלְחָן עוֹרֵךְ

LEADER:

Shulchan orech means "the set table." This is when the famous fifth question – "When do we eat?" – can be answered,

"Now!"

The seder plate is removed from the table.
When the meal is finished, children search for the afikoman.

25

Passover seder menu: Well-known Jewish singers often appeared at hotel seders. Jan Peerce (1904–1984), a Metropolitan Opera star, conducted the seder at the Deauville Hotel in Miami Beach, 1969.

11. TZAFUN — The Afikoman
צָפוּן

Pouch for
afikoman,
China, 19th century

The seder plate is returned to the table.

LEADER:

Tzafun means "hidden." Afikoman means "dessert." Since tradition tells us that neither the meal nor the seder can be concluded without finding and eating the hidden dessert, whoever finds it may demand a reward.

Children – Now is the time for you to negotiate your reward.
Parents and grandparents – **We need you!**

All eat the afikoman. The third cup of wine is filled.

26

12. BARECH — Blessing after the Meal
בָּרֵךְ

LEADER:

It is a mitzvah to say Grace after Meals. As it is written, "When you have eaten and are satisfied, you shall bless Adonai, your God, for the good land which God has given you."

ALL:

Praised are You, Adonai our God, Ruler of the Universe, who in goodness, mercy, and kindness gives food to the world.

Blessed is our God, whose food we have eaten and by whose goodness we live.

Praised are You, Adonai our God, who provides food for all life.

Blessed be Your Name forever in the mouth of every living thing.

Praised be the Creator of Life.

Seder show towel,
Alsace, France, 1821

בִּרְכַּת הַמָּזוֹן (Grace)

LEADER:	חֲבֵרַי נְבָרֵךְ
ALL:	יְהִי שֵׁם יְיָ מְבֹרָךְ מֵעַתָּה וְעַד עוֹלָם.
LEADER:	בִּרְשׁוּת מָרָנָן וְחַבֵּרַי, נְבָרֵךְ אֱלֹהֵינוּ שֶׁאָכַלְנוּ מִשֶּׁלוֹ.
ALL:	בָּרוּךְ אֱלֹהֵינוּ שֶׁאָכַלְנוּ מִשֶּׁלוֹ וּבְטוּבוֹ חָיִינוּ.

בָּרוּךְ אַתָּה יְיָ אֱלֹהֵינוּ מֶלֶךְ הָעוֹלָם הַזָּן אֶת הָעוֹלָם כֻּלוֹ
בְּטוּבוֹ, בְּחֵן בְּחֶסֶד וּבְרַחֲמִים. הוּא נוֹתֵן לֶחֶם לְכָל־בָּשָׂר, כִּי
לְעוֹלָם חַסְדּוֹ. וּבְטוּבוֹ הַגָּדוֹל תָּמִיד לֹא חָסַר לָנוּ, וְאַל יֶחְסַר
לָנוּ מָזוֹן לְעוֹלָם וָעֶד בַּעֲבוּר שְׁמוֹ הַגָּדוֹל. כִּי הוּא אֵל זָן וּמְפַרְנֵס
לַכֹּל, וּמֵטִיב לַכֹּל, וּמֵכִין מָזוֹן לְכָל בְּרִיּוֹתָיו אֲשֶׁר בָּרָא.
בָּרוּךְ אַתָּה יְיָ הַזָּן אֶת הַכֹּל.
כַּכָּתוּב וְאָכַלְתָּ וְשָׂבָעְתָּ וּבֵרַכְתָּ אֶת־יְיָ אֱלֹהֶיךָ עַל הָאָרֶץ
הַטּוֹבָה אֲשֶׁר נָתַן לָךְ. בָּרוּךְ אַתָּה יְיָ עַל הָאָרֶץ וְעַל הַמָּזוֹן.
וּבְנֵה יְרוּשָׁלַיִם עִיר הַקֹּדֶשׁ בִּמְהֵרָה בְיָמֵינוּ.
בָּרוּךְ אַתָּה יְיָ בּוֹנֵה בְרַחֲמָיו יְרוּשָׁלָיִם. אָמֵן.
הָרַחֲמָן הוּא יַנְחִילֵנוּ יוֹם שֶׁכֻּלוֹ טוֹב.
עֹשֶׂה שָׁלוֹם בִּמְרוֹמָיו, הוּא יַעֲשֶׂה שָׁלוֹם עָלֵינוּ וְעַל כָּל יִשְׂרָאֵל,
וְאִמְרוּ אָמֵן.

ALL:

We recall the third divine promise, "I will redeem you with an outstretched arm."

בָּרוּךְ אַתָּה יְיָ אֱלֹהֵינוּ מֶלֶךְ הָעוֹלָם בּוֹרֵא פְּרִי הַגָּפֶן.

Ba-ruch a-tah A-do-nai E-lo-hey-nu me-lech ha-o-lam bo-rey p'ri ha-ga-fen.

Blessed are You, Eternal God, Ruler of the Universe, who creates the fruit of the vine.

All drink the third cup of wine.

27

ELIYAHU

Kiddush cup,
Palestine, 20th century

ANY CHILD STILL AT THE TABLE :

There is an extra cup of wine at the table. This is the cup for Eliyahu. There is a tale that Eliyahu, or Elijah, a great ancient prophet who challenged rulers to live more justly, visits every seder to wish everyone a year of peace and freedom. As we open the door for Elijah, we recognize that Passover is a night for openness. We open our doors to visitors, our minds to learning and personal growth, and our hearts to those less fortunate.

The door is opened. Elijah's filled cup remains on the table.

⭐ Elijah's cup is filled before the door is opened. One tradition is to fill Elijah's cup by passing it around, allowing participants to pour a little wine from their cups into Elijah's. This reminds us that we must all do our part to make this a better world and assure our redemption.

ALL SING:

אֵלִיָּהוּ הַנָּבִיא, אֵלִיָּהוּ הַתִּשְׁבִּי, אֵלִיָּהוּ, אֵלִיָּהוּ, אֵלִיָּהוּ הַגִּלְעָדִי,
בִּמְהֵרָה בְיָמֵנוּ יָבֹא אֵלֵינוּ, עִם מָשִׁיחַ בֶּן דָּוִד, עִם מָשִׁיחַ בֶּן דָּוִד.

Eliyahu Hanavi

Watch Eliyahu's cup to see if any of the wine disappears.

The door is closed.

28

From the *Second Cincinnati Haggadah*, Amsterdam, ca. 1716

13. HALLEL — Praising God
הַלֵּל

? Many parts of the seder are structured in fours. How many can you name?

The fourth cup of wine is filled.

PARTICIPANT:

It is our duty to thank and praise, laud and glorify, extol and honor, exalt and adore God who performed all these miracles for our fathers and mothers and for us.

May it be Your will to bring all families who are suffering persecution into freedom as You brought our ancestors to freedom.

May we be worthy to enjoy the Passover holiday together with all the families of Israel in freedom and unity.

Amen.

29

14. NIRTZAH — Conclusion
נִרְצָה

PARTICIPANT:

As our seder draws to a close, we raise our cups of wine. The final cup recalls us to our covenant with the Eternal One, reminds us that tasks still await us as a people, and validates a great purpose for which the people of Israel live: the preservation and affirmation of hope.

ALL:

As it is written, "And I will take you to be my people."

בָּרוּךְ אַתָּה יְיָ אֱלֹהֵינוּ מֶלֶךְ הָעוֹלָם בּוֹרֵא פְּרִי הַגָּפֶן.

Ba-ruch a-tah A-do-nai E-lo-hey-nu me-lech ha-o-lam bo-rey p'ri ha-ga-fen.

Blessed are You, Eternal God, Ruler of the Universe, who creates the fruit of the vine.

All drink the fourth cup of wine.

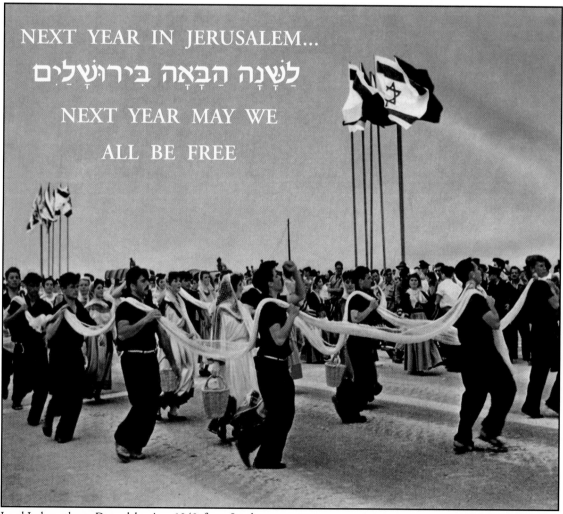

Israel Independence Day celebration, 1948, from *Israel*

From the film *The Animated Haggadah*, Rony Oren, 1985

 Many feel this ancient Aramaic song is best sung faster and faster with each verse.

Chad Gadya

With Spirit

Chad gad - ya,_____ chad gad - ya, di —

z' van a - ba bit - rei— zu - zei. Chad gad - ya,_____

chad gad - ya. *First verse:* V'_____ a - ta shun - ra v' a chal l' gad-ya di —

Fine

2nd verse: V'_____ a - ta chal - ba v' na shach l' shun - ra d' a - chal l' gad -

3rd verse: ya di— V'_____ a - ta chut - ra v'hi-kah l' chal - ba d'_____

(verses 4-9 as above)

na - shach l' shun - ra d'— a - chal l' gad - ya di —

31

ONE LITTLE GOAT

There was one little goat. One very little goat that my father bought for two zuzim...
One little goat, One very little goat.

Then came a cat and ate the goat that my father bought for two zuzim...
One little goat, One very little goat.

Then came a dog and bit the cat that ate the goat that my father bought for two zuzim...
One little goat, One very little goat.

Then came a stick and beat the dog that bit the cat that ate the goat that my father bought for two zuzim...
One little goat, One very little goat.

Then came a fire and burned the stick that beat the dog that bit the cat that ate the goat that my father bought for two zuzim...
One little goat, One very little goat.

From *Haggadah* - Hamburg, 1740/41

Then came the water and quenched the fire that burned the stick that beat the dog that bit the cat that ate the goat that my father bought for two zuzim...
One little goat, One very little goat.

Then came the ox and drank the water that quenched the fire that burned the stick that beat the dog that bit the cat that ate the goat that my father bought for two zuzim...
One little goat, One very little goat.

Then came the slaughterer and slaughtered the ox that drank the water that quenched the fire that burned the stick that beat the dog that bit the cat that ate the goat that my father bought for two zuzim...
One little goat, One very little goat.

Then came the angel of death and killed the slaughterer who slaughtered the ox that drank the water that quenched the fire that burned the stick that beat the dog that bit the cat that ate the goat that my father bought for two zuzim...
One little goat, One very little goat.

Then came the Holy One, blessed be God's name, and God slew the angel of death who killed the slaughterer who slaughtered the ox that drank the water that quenched the fire that burned the stick that beat the dog that bit the cat that ate the goat that my father bought for two zuzim...
One little goat, One very little goat.

("Chad Gadya" - Aramaic - continued)

(verse)

4th. V'a-ta nu-ra v'sa-raf l'chut-ra d'hi-kah l'chal-ba d'na-shach l'shun-ra d'a-chal l'gad-ya di-z'van a-ba bit-rei zu-zei...
Chad gad-ya, chad gad-ya.

5th. V'a-ta ma-ya v'cha-vah l'nu-ra d'sa-raf l'chut-ra d'hi-kah l'chal-ba d'na-shach l'shun-ra d'a-chal l'gad-ya di-z'van a-ba bit-rei zu-zei...
Chad gad-ya, chad gad-ya.

6th. V'a-ta to-ra v'sha-ta l'ma-ya d'cha-vah l'nu-ra d'sa-raf l'chut-ra d'hi-kah l'chal-ba d'na-shach l'shun-ra d'a-chal l'gad-ya di-z'van a-ba bit-rei zu-zei...
Chad gad-ya, chad gad-ya.

7th. V'a-ta ha-sho-cheit v'sha-chat l'to-ra d'sha-ta l'ma-ya d'cha-vah l'nu-ra d'sa-raf l'chut-ra d'hi-kah l'chal-ba d'na-shach l'shun-ra d'a-chal l'gad-ya di-z'van a-ba bit-rei zu-zei...
Chad gad-ya, chad gad-ya.

8th. V'a-ta mal'ach ha-ma-vet v'sha-chat l'sho-cheit d'sha-chat l'to-ra d'sha-ta l'ma-ya d'cha-vah l'nu-ra d'sa-raf l'chut-ra d'hi-kah l'chal-ba d'na-shach l'shun-ra d'a-chal l'gad-ya di-z'van a-ba bit-rei zu-zei...
Chad gad-ya, chad gad-ya.

9th. V'a-ta Ha-ka-dosh ba-ruch Hu v'sha-chat l'mal'ach ha-ma-vet d'sha-chat l'sho-cheit d'sha-chat l'to-ra d'sha-ta l'ma-ya d'cha-vah l'nu-ra d'sa-raf l'chut-ra d'hi-kah l'chal-ba d'na-shach l'shun-ra d'a-chal l'gad-ya di-z'van a-ba bit-rei zu-zei...
Chad gad-ya, chad gad-ya.

SOURCES

Cover. *The Seder*
Meichel Pressman, 1950.
Watercolor on paper, 12.2"x18.5".
The Jewish Museum, New York.

(indexed by page number)

ii. *Second Cincinnati Haggadah*
Amsterdam, ca. 1716.
Hebrew Union College – Jewish Institute of Religion
(HUC – JIR), Klau Library, Cincinnati.
This extraordinary Haggadah includes oil miniatures on
parchment inspired by engravings found in the printed
Amsterdam Haggadah of 1712.

1. *Spanish Haggadah*
Spain, ca. 1350-1360.
British Library, London.
The "Ha Lachma Anya" ceremony shows the father placing a
basket of matzot on the head of a child. It was then placed
successively on the heads of each participant. The illuminations
in this Haggadah, typical of Sephardic Haggadot, emphasized
ceremonial rites of the holiday.

2. *Haggadah for Passover*
Hebrew Publishing Co., New York, 1921.
This seder scene is the first illustration in this popular Hebrew
and English Haggadah. Note the leader's cushion, wine, candles,
and the pitcher of water being carried to the table for "Urchatz."

5. Tiered Seder Plate
Vienna, 1814.
Silver, cast, pierced, and engraved, 14.75"x16".
Franz Strobl (?), active 1811-1843.
Hebrew Union College Skirball Cultural Center and Museum,
Los Angeles.
This seder plate includes three tiers for matzot. Such tiering
was a signature feature of plates in 19th-century Europe. The
central figure is Elijah.

6. Kiddush cup from *The Haggadah*
Arthur Szyk, 1965.
"Massadah" and "Alumoth," Jerusalem and Tel Aviv.
Reprinted with the permission of The Arthur Szyk Society and
Alexandra Bracie. (1200 Edgehill Dr., Burlingame, CA 94010).
This modern illuminated Haggadah was termed "the most
beautiful book ever published by human hands" by the *London
Times*. 250 copies on vellum were produced in its first release
in 1939. The Haggadah was popularized in a velvet-covered
edition in the 1960s.

7. *First Cincinnati Haggadah*
Southern Germany, ca. 1480-90.
HUC – JIR, Klau Library, Cincinnati.
This typical Ashkenazic illuminated manuscript has illustrations in
the margins including both biblical scenes and holiday rites. This
marginal image, seen close up, is of a seated Rabbi Eliezer ben Azariah.

8. Matzah comb
Germany, 18th-19th century.
Iron, 8.75"x17.5".
The baking of matzah was and is carefully supervised so that the
dough does not rise. To hasten baking and prevent rising, the
surface is pierced by the spikes of a matzah roller or "comb."

8. Matzah bag
Moravia, 1904.
Jewish Museum, Mikulov (Nikolsburg), Moravia.
Velvet, embroidered with cotton, cotton and metallic fringe,
cotton cord, linen damask lining, 17.5"x12.5".
A sectional bag with three compartments was in common use
in Ashkenazic communities in Europe in the early 1900s. The
embroidery included names for the symbols of the holiday
and ceremonies of the seder.

9. *The Haggadah*
Arthur Szyk, 1965.
"Massadah" and "Alumoth," Jerusalem and Tel Aviv.
Reprinted with the permission of The Arthur Szyk Society
and Alexandra Bracie.
This magnificent mem, the first letter of the "Mah Nishtanah"
depicts the talent and genius of the calligrapher/artist. In the
spirit of his medieval predecessors, Szyk beautifully integrated
calligraphy, narrative, illumination, and illustration to lead a
modern resurgence of manuscript illumination.

10. *Passover Haggadah*
Darmstadt, Germany, 1733.
From facsimile, W. Turnowsky Ltd., Tel Aviv.
Original: Jewish National and University Library, Jerusalem.
The artist and scribe, Joseph ben David Aharon of Leipnik,
painted in rich, warm colors. Illustrations were copied from
well-known printed Haggadot from Prague (1526), Mantua
(1560), Venice (1601), and Amsterdam (1695). Costumes,
backgrounds, and some detail were altered to suit the 18th-
century German style. This manuscript is typical of those
commissioned by wealthy Jews for themselves or in honor
of their loved ones.

11. *Barcelona Haggadah*
Barcelona, mid-14th century.
The *Barcelona Haggadah* represents the type of Spanish
Haggadah with full-size illustrations within the text, as
compared to *The Golden Haggadah,* which has miniature
illustrations. Illustrations are biblical, ritual, or textual as
in this rendition of "Avadim Hayinu."

12. *The Golden Haggadah*
Spain, probably Barcelona, ca. 1320.
British Library, London.
The Golden Haggadah is one of seventeen ancient Haggadot
found in Spain. Full-page miniatures, in ink and gold leaf on
vellum, present biblical scenes of Genesis and Exodus:
Top Lft. – Aaron greets Moses and his wife, Tzipporah;
Top Rt. – Angel of the burning bush, Moses with shoes on
and off; *Bot. Lft.* – Moses and Aaron speak before Pharaoh and
two counselors; *Bot. Rt.* – Aaron holds the snake while Moses
announces the miracle to gathering Jews.

13. "The Four Sons" from *Song of David / The Moss Haggadah*
David Moss, 1980.
Courtesy of: Bet Alpha Editions, PO Box 12711,
Berkeley, CA 94712.
David Moss was commissioned in 1980 by Richard and
Beatrice Levy to create a handwritten, illuminated Haggadah
for their personal collection. These four images are but a few
of many remarkable acrylic paintings intermingled with the
unique calligraphy of this exemplary modern Haggadah.

14. *The Haggadah of Passover*
Sigmund Forst, 1955.
Shulsinger Bros. Linotyping & Publishing Co., New York.
Illustrated Haggadot in the 1950s often depicted artists' renditions of biblical scenes. The colors and images are striking and memorable.

15. *Haggadah of Passover*
Dr. Joseph Loewy and Joseph Guens, after 1945.
Sinai Publishing, Tel Aviv.
Post-World War II illustrated Haggadot included black & white and colorized etchings and paintings depicting midrashic interpretations of Bible stories. In addition to traditional text, this issue has detailed commentary, ritual instructions, and even musical scores. The cover includes a copper insert of a scene of Israel.

16. *Haggadah of Passover*
Illustrations by Marc Chagall, 1987.
Leon Amiel Publisher, New York and Paris.
The Chagall Haggadah paintings, originally commissioned more than 25 years prior to the publication of the Haggadah, include the world-famous "Story of Exodus" illustrated series.

19. "Parting of the Red Sea" from *Passover Haggadah*
Raphael Abecassis, 1993.
Razim Art, Netanya, Israel.
Raphael Abecassis's unique Passover paintings were photographed by Nissim Lev and intermingled with his beautifully transcribed text. This well-known and prolific Moroccan artist has produced four distinct Haggadot, each with a slightly different emphasis and style.

20. *Sarajevo Haggadah*
Barcelona, 14th century.
The *Sarajevo Haggadah* is perhaps the best-known Hebrew illuminated manuscript. Full-page miniatures illustrate Bible stories from Creation through Moses blessing the Israelites. This Haggadah, originally of Spanish origin, made its way to Italy in 1492 and eventually to the National Museum in Sarajevo. The Nazis tried to confiscate the well-known book, but the manuscript was hidden away by the director of the museum.

21. *Birds' Head Haggadah*
Southern Germany, ca. 1300.
The *Birds' Head* is the oldest extant German illuminated Haggadah. The figures are dressed in medieval German-Jewish garb, including the infamous "Jew's Hat" the Jews were forced to wear by the Church. The heads of Jews are replaced by those of birds to avoid any chance that a figure might be taken as a graven image. Other distortions such as blank faces or heads covered by helmets were also used.

23. Matzah cover
Jerusalem, early 20th century.
Velvet, silk & metallic embroidery, shells, sequins, fish scales.
HUC Skirball Cultural Center and Museum, Los Angeles.

24. *Making Haroset*
Toby Knobel Fluek, Czernica, 1975.
Oil on canvas, 16"x20".
The painting presents the ingredients and tools needed to make charoset. Fluek, a Czernica resident, fled the city during the time of occupation and deportation during World War II and hid for the duration of the war.

25. *First Seder in Jerusalem*
Reuven Rubin, 1950.
Oil on canvas, 10.5"x64".
Reuven Rubin Museum, Tel Aviv.
Rubin was born in Romania and emigrated to Israel in 1955. This colorful painting of a seder scene depicts the walls of the Old City in the background with figures around the table representing varied Jewish communities or regions. All share in the hope for a peaceful future.

26. Seder menu from *American Heritage Haggadah*
Edited by D. Geffen, 1992.
Geffen Publishing House, Jerusalem and New York.

26. Pouch for afikoman
China, 19th century.
Cotton, satin, embroidery thread, gold thread, diam 5.75".
HUC Skirball Cultural Center and Museum, Los Angeles.
This small yet colorful pouch held the piece of matzah for the afikoman.

27. Seder show towel
Alsace, France, 1821.
Linen, embroidered with silk thread and silk ribbon, 50"x15.5".
HUC Skirball Cultural Center and Museum, Los Angeles, gift of Rabbi Folkman.
This embroidered towel was placed by the door in Alsatian homes to cover soiled towels used for the seder handwashing. The towels were known as Sederwehl in the Judeo-Alsatian dialect.

28. Kiddush cup
Palestine, 20th century.
Ceramic, h 3.75", d 2.6".
HUC Skirball Cultural Center and Museum, Los Angeles.

29. *Second Cincinnati Haggadah*
Amsterdam, ca. 1716.
HUC – JIR, Klau Library, Cincinnati.
The scribe was Wolf Loeb of Trebitsch. This elegant seder scene is of a wealthy Jewish household in Amsterdam, ca. 1700.

30. Photograph from *Israel*
Editors: A.B. Harman and Yigael Yadin, 1958.
Massadah Publishing Co., Tel Aviv and Jerusalem.
This colorful photo was taken on Independence Day, 1948.

31. *The Animated Haggadah*
Rony Oren, 1985.
Scopus Films, Woodhaven, New York.
This "Chad Gadya" scene is a photo of a creation in clay, modeled by Rony Oren for the delightful children's film *The Animated Haggadah*.

32. *Haggadah*
Hamburg, 1740/41.
HUC – JIR, Klau Library, Cincinnati.
The *Hamburg's* oil miniatures follow illustrations from the 1712 *Amsterdam Haggadah* but utilize a folk-art style found in other 18th-century Haggadot. This miniature goat scene accompanies the traditional Aramaic song "Chad Gadya."

Contemporary photographs and drawings by Elie M. Gindi.

We are delighted that you have shared tonight's seder with us. Please write your name and the date below. Write down your favorite part or picture or leave a comment. As the list grows, look at the names and notes from the people who have used this Haggadah before you.

DATE	NAME	COMMENTS